SURVIVING
NORWAY'S
NAZI
OCCUPATION
AND THE
KOREAN
WAR

SURVIVING NORWAY'S
NAZI
OCCUPATION
AND THE
KOREAN
WAR

SVERRE WAAGEN

nordic
PUBLISHING
Prior Lake, Minnesota

Nordic Publishing, LLC
P. O. Box 923, Prior Lake, MN 55372
www.NordicPublishing.biz

nordic
PUBLISHING

ISBN: 978-0-9903788-1-5

Cover design: Christopher Edmund, christopheredmund@outlook.com
Interior design: Dorie McClelland, springbookdesign.com

Printed in the United States of America
First printing, 2014

DEDICATION

This book is dedicated to my mother, Gyda Waagen, who never left Norway, my father, Gabriel Waagen, who bravely went to America in search of a better life, and my sisters, Petra (Waagen) Clausen who moved to Sweden, Elly (Waagen) Brevik who moved to Fosnavag, Norway, and Gerd Waagen, who resides in Seattle, Washington, and is the reason I left Norway to come to America.

My life story starts in Norway but ends in America. The book is also dedicated to my wife, Alice Haase Waagen, my children, Rose Marie (Waagen) Meuwissen, Linda (Waagen) Hamilton, Norman Waagen, Sonja (Waagen) Gunter, Paul Waagen, Richard Waagen, my grandchildren and great-grandchildren.

And lastly, but not least, to all the soldiers still fighting today, those who fought in past wars, and my fellow soldiers who fought beside me in Korea and Japan. Some lived to tell their stories and some never made it back to tell theirs, so this one is for them.

Contents

BACK IN JAPAN

BACK IN THE UNITED STATES

WAR HUMOR

WAR MEMORIBILIA

NAZI OCCUPATION OF NORWAY

Norway Flag.

Ja, Vi Elsker Dette Landet

Ja, vi elsker dette landet,
som det stiger frem,
furet, værbitt over vannet,
med de tusen hjem—
elsker, elsker det og tenker
på vår far og mor
og den saganatt som senker
drømmer på vår jord.
Og den saganatt som senker,
senker drømmer på vår jord.

Yes, We Love This Country

Yes, we love this country
as it rises forth,
rugged, weathered, above the sea,
with the thousands of homes.
Love, love it and think
of our father and mother
and the saga night that sends
dreams to our earth.
And the saga night that sends,
dreams to our earth.

View of fjords in Gursken, Norway.

LIVING IN NORWAY DURING WWII

My dad, Gabriel Vagen, went to America in 1910. He made good money there and he came back to Norway about 1920. He got married a short time after that. He remodeled an old house there and built a new barn. They had two cows, three sheep and some chickens. That was about the average size farm people had around there.

He and another man bought a fishing boat. He caught lots of Cod fishing with nets and they would catch lots of Cod up North in Lofoten, Norway. This went good for two or three years and then all of a sudden there were no more Cod to fish. And he went broke. His partner fell overboard when the boat was anchored in Vagen fjord and drowned.

I was born in Gursken, Norway, on November 9, 1927, the son of Gyda and Gabriel Vagen.

In 1927, he left for America again. He served in the U.S. Army in the 1st World War and he became a U.S. citizen. If he stayed out of the U. S. more than seven years, you lost your citizenship. So that is the reason he left for America again. He was lucky this time and made good money.

He was a streetcar conductor in Minneapolis for some time. He also had a hotel in St. Paul together with another man who was a neighbor of his in Norway.

But this time he was more careful with his money—he put it all in the bank. But then the depression came in the early thirties and the banks went broke and he lost all his money. And then the tough times came. I remember he told me that he had to work in the fields to pick corn sixteen hours a day and made fifty cents a day.

It was a very tough time for him now. He sent whatever money he had to Norway to support his family. Then the 2nd World War started.

We got some letters from him at first, but they were first read by the Nazi Germans. And then there was no letters or correspondence with the U.S. at all. We did not know if he was still living and he did not know if we were living for over five years.

The occupation of Norway started April 9, 1940, and lasted until May 8, 1945.

I was twelve years old when the Nazi Germans entered Norway. We woke up in the morning on April 9, 1940, and we were told Nazi Germany had made a sneak attack on Norway during the night and we were under German Nazi Occupation. The Nazi Germans took over some buildings in Larsness, Norway, not far from us. They took over all the newspapers and everything we were told was all propaganda. Then we were told to turn in all our radios and, if you did not, the penalty was jail or in some cases death. The Norwegian soldiers went north and got organized. They battled the Nazi Germans for about two months but finally had to give up. The Nazi Germans had a strong army and were well trained.

The Norwegians were a peaceful nation and did not expect anything like that to happen. The Nazi Germans had Merchant ships in every port of Norway. But every ship had soldiers on board, not merchandise. They all came out at the same time and took over the country during the night.

Right away we got ration cards and you could buy very little of anything. In Gursken we did not have any electricity so we had to use kerosene lamps. We got five liters per month and that came out to about two hours per day for one lamp. So we were in the dark the rest of the time. We had no TV, no radio. There was not much we could do, especially in the winter when it got dark at 3 p.m. and it got light about 10 a.m.

We had one wood stove in the living room and that was all. I slept upstairs. I had two cement stones we heated on the stove and rolled in newspaper and put in the bed to warm it up. On the weekend if we were really lucky, I got ahold of a good book and a candle. I left my mittens on. It got very cold in the winter and we had lots of snow. Sometimes the road would be closed for three weeks. They did not have very good equipment to work with in those days. So to go any place you had to go on skis or use a row boat. We did not have any outboard motors like we have today.

This was a very difficult time for the people of Norway. Food got scarce. I remember times when all we had for supper was rock salt and potatoes.

A WWII bomb shelter in Drøbak, Norway.

7

Nazis attacking the Oscarsborg fortress, in the Oslofjord, Norway, near Drøbak where the Norwegians sank the German heavy cruiser Blücher *on 9 April 1940.*

Oscarsborg fortress opened to the public in 2003.

OCCUPIED NORWAY — SCHOOLS AND CHURCHES CLOSED

I remember in 1941, Norway got orders to close all the schools. It was during the winter in January, the teachers all had to go to Oslo and have a fast course in the German language and learn some new things they had to teach the children about the Nazi and Hitler ways. It was a very scary time for teachers. The schools were closed for about three months. As children we did not like school much, but when the school was closed we really missed it. And when the school opened up again we all liked school.

Shortly thereafter, Norway was ordered to close all the churches. The Nazi Germans had set a certain date for the churches to close. So the week before the closings we held church services every day until the closing date. I don't remember how long they were closed. I believe it was about three months. The head of the church, the Bishops, had many meetings with the Nazi Germans and finally the churches were re-opened. Some of the heads of the churches were sent to jail and one was sent to a German Nazi concentration camp in Germany. It was a very dark time in Norway during that time.

At this time we were told to cover every window. No light from the house could be seen from the outside. If it was, the Nazi German soldiers would come knock at the door and give us a warning ticket. We did not have any blinds, so we had to make window coverings out of old paper bags or else sit in the dark. If we had any radios we had to turn them in to the Nazi Germans. The penalty for keeping one was jail or in some cases death.

We did have newspapers, but we could not believe anything printed in them. It was only what the Nazi Germans wanted us to know. The

Nazi Germans were winning on every war front and they always shot down lots of American planes. The Nazi Germans never lost any. It was all propaganda, but most of us knew it.

Some of the big fishing boats were allowed to have a radio during the herring season, so they could keep track of where to catch the herring. The Nazi Germans wanted them to try to catch as many herring as possible because they needed the oil from the herring for glycerin to make explosives for the war.

We had ration cards for everything. But there was very little to buy. The flour we got to make bread was bad; the bread would not get done. The bottom part of the bread would not get baked and the upper part would just crumble. But we had to eat it anyway. We ate lots of salted herring along with other fish and potatoes. We also had some carrots and rutabagas that we could grow on the farm. Blueberries grew wild in the mountains and we would pick them to eat. We made blueberry juice from them so they would last thru the winter. We did a lot of fishing but many times we did not catch any. So then we'd go back to the salted herring or dried herring and the potatoes.

Sverre Waagen's family farm in Gursken, Norway,
where he lived during WWII.

THE EARLY PART OF THE WAR

In the early part of the war, some people had radios and we could get Norwegian stations that really talked against the Nazi Germans. The news came on at seven every night and they told the truth about the war. The Nazi Germans could not figure out where this station was located. This went on for months. It was two men who did the war news broadcast. They had the whole radio station packed in suitcases and they were in a different place every night. That is why the Nazi Germans could not find them. They traveled from Larsness to Hareid on the same bus that the Nazi Germans were on and even sat together with the Nazi German soldiers. Their suitcases with the broadcasting equipment were with them on the same bus, also. But they finally had to quit broadcasting because it was getting extremely dangerous.

Norway had lots of underground soldiers. During the day they worked their regular jobs and at night they did all kinds of sabotage missions. After the war was over they wore their own uniforms and took over the German Nazi camps.

This helped the Americans and the English. Mainly, because it took lots of soldiers to do all this work after the war was over. Norway is a small country but they did their part to help in many ways. After the war, Norway sent many soldiers to help out in occupied Germany.

All the Norwegian Nazis were rounded up and jailed after the war. Later they were sent to court and sentenced according to what crimes they had committed during the war.

Quisling, the biggest traitor, lived in Oslo and was running Norway during the war for the Nazis. He was just a puppet. He had to do what the Nazi Germans told him to do. He was arrested right away after the war and was executed at the Akershus in Oslo, Norway. He was considered Norway's biggest traitor. Terboven, the German Nazi, who was over him, took a pill and killed himself before the Norwegians could get to him. Otherwise, he probably would have been executed at the Akershus, too.

Akershus fortress at the Akershus in Oslo, Norway, where Vidkun Quisling was executed.

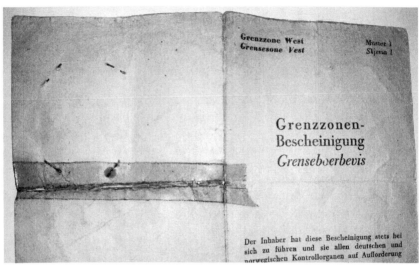

Grenzzone West
Grensesone Vest

Muster 1
Skjema 1

Grenzzonen-
Bescheinigung
Grenseboerbevis

Der Inhaber hat diese Bescheinigung stets bei
sich zu führen und sie allen deutschen und
norwegischen Kontrollorganen auf Aufforderung

GRENZZONEN-BESCHEINIGUNG
Grenzzone West

GRENSEBOERBEVIS
Grensesone Vest

Nr.: 3601

Polizeidirektor/Lensmann in
Politimesteren/Lensmannen i

Inhaber dieser Grenzzonen-Bescheinigung,
Innehaveren av dette grenseboerbevis

Vaagen, Sverre   geb. am   in
                        født den   *i*

Beruf: Staatsangehörigkeit:
Yrke: *Nasjonalitet:*

hat seinen/ihren ständigen Wohnsitz in:
har sin faste bopel i:

Polizei/Lensmanns-Bezirk:
Politi/lensmanns-distrikt:

Diese Bescheinigung berechtigt zum Verkehr in folgenden Polizei-
bezirken der Grenzzone West:
*Dette bevis gir innehaveren rett til å ferdes i følgende politi-
distrikter i Grensesone Vest:*

Ort: Vågsøy lensmannsktr. Måløy Siegel
Sted: Stempel
Datum:
Datum:

Sverre Wågen
Eigenhändige Unterschrift
Egenhendig underskrift

Unterschrift des Polizeidirektors bzw.
Lensmanns
*Politimesteren eller lensmannens
underskrift*

14

FIXING THE MINE BELT

My uncle, Oscar Venoy, and I were fishing shrimp when the Nazi Germans took over our fishing boat and us. The boat was 35 feet long and had a place to sleep and cook below deck. I was to do most of the cooking. But, now we had to go where the Nazi Germans told us to go. The weather had been very stormy for the past few days.

We were at Askvoll in the beginning of the Sogne Fjordane. The Nazi Germans had many mine belts out there, but the storm had loosened some of the mines. We were ordered, along with some Nazi German soldiers, to go out, get the lost mines and fasten them to the belts again. This was a dangerous job especially in bad weather. My uncle was very good at handling the boat during storms. We got the mines, brought them to the belts and the Nazi German soldiers fastened them back on the belts. I was very glad when that job was done. The mines have horns and if you accidentally hit the horns they explode. But we made it through that day.

Sometimes we had to get supplies for the soldiers, like when they needed bread. We would ask them for a loaf of bread for ourselves and we each got one. This really helped us with the ration cards. Other times we carried lumber and building supplies on our boat. But sometimes we ended up in a German Nazi Warship convoy. This was very dangerous because the Americans and the English would bomb or torpedo the convoy. We saw that happen a few times, but luckily we were not in those convoys. Sometimes we had to go out after the bombings and look for soldiers who were still alive. Other times we had to take supplies to the Nazi German camps where the soldiers were located. We saw lots of Russian prisoners at the Nazi German camps. We gave the prisoners dried herring when the guards were not looking. The prisoners were always looking for food. They would put it under their clothes so nobody would see it and eat it later.

SHOPPING IN ÅLESUND
DURING WWII

In order to buy clothes and things like that we had to go to Ålesund, Norway. We had to get up at 5 a.m. and get ready to take the bus to Hareid. Then take the ferry boat to Ålesund where sometimes the stores were closed and sometimes they did not have anything left. But you had to try because maybe you would get lucky.

The clothes were not very good. I remember one time I got a suit for my confirmation at church—the first one I ever got. It was black with white stripes. I was very proud of the suit. But one time I got caught in the rain and the suit turned a kind of grey color. It was ruined.

We arrived in Ålesund about 9 a.m. We had to run to the stores to see if they still had anything left. Well, we barely got in a store when the sirens went off. So then we had to go downstairs to the bomb shelter. Norway got bombed often by the English and American bombers because there were so many Nazi Germans in Norway. The Nazi Germans had large artillery guns and many Nazi Warship destroyers in Ålesund and that was what the English and Americans were trying to destroy. But sometimes they missed and hit the buildings in Ålesund. Every time a bomb exploded, the whole building we were in shook. The shelter was full of people. Some were crying and some were praying. We were all scared to death, but finally the sirens would come back on and that meant the bombings were over, for that time anyway. We all got out of there right away. I could see two or three buildings burning and the fire department was there trying to get the fires out. One building was gone but still smoking.

We had to catch the ferry at 3 p.m. to get on our way back home. We did not have any time left to go to another store. This was the way it was most of the time when we went shopping in Ålesund during the war in Norway.

Well, we finally got back to Hareid and got on the bus to go home. We got home about 7 p.m. that day, but we did not get any shopping done. This gives you an idea of what life was like in Norway during the war.

Old Norwegian milk maid hyttes on the mountain side.

TRYING TO ESCAPE
NAZI OCCUPIED NORWAY

During the Nazi German Occupation of Norway, the Nazi Germans took over our fishing boats and us. So we had no choice but to work for the Nazi Germans. We spent lots of time working around Måløy and Askvoll. It happened often that smaller fishing boats about 35 feet and similar in size would try to take their families with them and try to escape to England. The Nazi Germans were aware of this and were on the lookout for these types of boats. If the Nazi Germans caught them, they would kill all of them or else maybe they would be sent to Nazi German Concentration Camps. This was a very risky thing to do. Many made it, but many did not. The families of the ones that did not make it to England, if there were any left in Norway, would be gathered up and sent to jail or sent to the Nazi German Concentration Camps. So it was very risky to try to do this. Some of the men who made it, joined the Norwegian Army that had been started in England.

In 1943, we were in Måløy. I was 16 years old then, and knew somebody who had a boat and was planning to escape to England. This was top secret and they wanted me to go along. It was two boys in their twenties and I was all set to go with them. We were planning to leave the next day. But somehow my Uncle, Oscar Venoy, found out about it and would not let me go. The other boys left early the next day, without me.

After the war, we found out they made it half way to England before they had motor trouble. They ended up drifting north for days. Finally, an English Destroyer found them. They were picked up and were in very bad shape, but they made it.

Hard telling what would have happened to me if I had gone along. I wanted to get to England so I could get to America to find my father.

Well, I got to England and then America, but that was after the war. Soon after I arrived in America, I ended up as a U.S. soldier in the Korean War and then an Occupation soldier in Japan, but eventually I made it back to America.

Sverre Waagen and his sister, Elly Waagen, in Norway after the war ended.

Sverre Waagen's mother, Gyda Waagen, in Norway.

COMING TO AMERICA

UNITED STATES OF AMERICA
NATIONAL ANTHEM

O say can you see by the dawn's early light,
What so proudly we hailed at the twilight's last gleaming,
Whose broad stripes and bright stars through the perilous fight,
O'er the ramparts we watched, were so gallantly streaming?
And the rockets' red glare, the bombs bursting in air,
Gave proof through the night that our flag was still there;
O say does that star-spangled banner yet wave,
O'er the land of the free and the home of the brave?

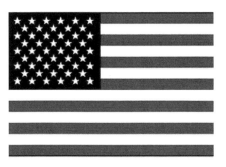

U.S. Flag.

THE DAY I LEFT GURSKEN

I was working with another man digging the foundation for a house when I got a telephone call from my sister, Gerd, who worked in Oslo. There was only one telephone for the town and the lady who had the telephone had to walk two blocks to tell me I had a telephone call. I had to walk two blocks back to get to the telephone. It was my sister, Gerd. She said she could get a ticket to America on a troop transport ship. The ship had taken soldiers to Europe and was taking passengers on its way back to New York. We had been talking about going to the U.S. for some time. It was the Oslo Fjord and the Bergen Fjord ships that usually took passengers to New York. They were booked full for about two years ahead. So this was our chance. I had to make up my mind there and then. I said, "Yes." I had to be in Oslo in seven days to board the ship. Gerd was going to get the passports ready. In Oslo you could get them ready in a hurry and she knew where to get it done.

I went back to my job and said I was quitting. I told them I was going to America. They looked at me. They thought I was crazy. But I picked up my tools and left. I went home and found an old suitcase, packed a few things, and left the next morning at 5 a.m. on the bus to Ålesund. Then, I took another bus to the train station and got on the train to Oslo. Everything went fine in Oslo. I had not been to a big city before.

Gerd and I got ready and boarded the troop transport ship. I believe the name of the ship was *Marine Jumper*. The ship went to England first and took aboard some more passengers and then we sailed for New York. The weather was pretty good for most of the time except for two days it was not so good. Those days we all got sick, but not too bad. It took about 11 days until we docked in New York. The Statue of Liberty was something we first saw in the harbor and we all were amazed to see it.

23

Marine Jumper is the ship Sverre Waagen and his sister, Gerd Waagen, booked passage to America on after WWII ended.

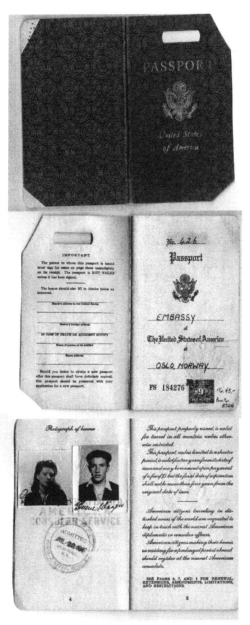

Joint United States of America passport for Sverre Waagen and Gerd Waagen used to book passage to America.

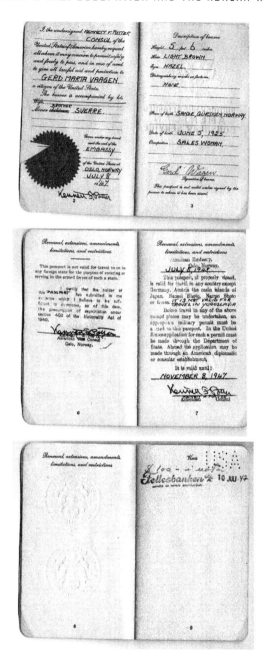

HOT SPRINGS

I could not speak much English and could hardly make a sentence go together. I had $50 in my pocket and we had to get a train to Hot Springs, South Dakota. The police were very helpful and got us on the train.

This was in the middle of July and it was very hot. I had been told it was very cold in South Dakota so I had woolen under clothes on and a wool suit. When we got to Hot Springs, South Dakota, it was 105 degrees. I could have killed that person who told me it was so cold there. Maybe that person had been there in January.

We got a hotel room and got some sleep. While we were on the way there, our dad had a heart attack and was in the V.A. Hospital. We got to see him, but he was not doing very well, so of course we did not get any help from him.

My sister, Gerd, could speak some English so she got a job working for some old lady. So she was okay. I on the other hand could not get any job because nobody wanted somebody who could not speak English. My dad knew a lady by the name of Clara who said she would help teach me English, so every evening I went there for about two hours. She was very good and helpful. I was learning English fast, but I was broke. I found a room that was cheaper to rent.

Some Norwegian lady who worked for some people who worked at the V. A. Hospital said they needed someone to pull weeds in their garden. I did the job and got $5.00. This was in 1947. This was the first money I made in the U.S.A. A few days later I got a job at the Sisters Catholic Hospital to run the laundry machine. I would get $70 per month and one meal a day.

Where the hospital was located, was near a large river running right through town. Sometime earlier that year the river flooded over and water got in the basement of the hospital. There was red clay everywhere. There were many rooms down there and they said if I would clean one up, I could sleep there. I cleaned for days and they put a bed down there for me. I was happy for now. I had a job, a room, one meal a day and $70 per month.

At the Sister's Catholic Hospital laundry, they had a problem saying my name, Sverre. Some Indian girl started calling me, Johnny, so I started answering to that name. I was still learning English from Clara. I was 19 years old at that time. The lady was about 30 years old and she had a sister who was a lot younger. But the problem was that they both were the most beautiful girls I had ever seen. I had to quit taking English lessons because of this. I could not take being around such beautiful girls.

My dad did not get better. He died in January of 1948, at the age of 59.

*Gabriel Waagen's headstone at the VA Cemetery
in Hot Springs, South Dakota.*

Gabriel Waagen in his uniform from WWI.

Gabriel Waagen
(Name)
January 26, 1948
(Date of Death)
Mech. Cav. Det. 39   163rd O.D.
Enlisted 1-26-198 Honorably Discharged 1-15-1919
10   7   16
(Section)   (Row)   (Grave No.)

VETERANS ADMINISTRATION CEMETERY
Veterans Administration Facility, Hot Springs, South Dakota

VETERANS ADMINISTRATION FACILITY
of
HOT SPRINGS, SOUTH DAKOTA

THE PRINT on the front of this folder is a sectional view of the Cemetery at the Veterans Administration Facility, Hot Springs, South Dakota, and is sent to you so that you can visualize the last resting place of your relative.

At present, there are more than eight hundred veterans of the armed forces in this cemetery. Included in that number are veterans of all the most recent wars in which this country has engaged, as well as many soldiers from the regular Army, Navy and Marine Corps.

The cemetery is situated between rolling hills characteristic of this portion of our country and is partially surrounded by native trees and shrubs. Much effort is expended in maintaining the cemetery and this care will continue so long as the Government exists. A marble headstone, exactly like those marking the graves of his fellows, will be placed upon the grave of your relative. The headstone will bear his name, the date of his death and the military organization of which he was a member. On Memorial Day a flag is placed on each grave and commemorative services are conducted in the cemetery in tribute to the Nation's dead heroes. Bronze tablets bearing the Gettysburg Address, The Declaration of Independence, "The Bivouac of the Dead", and other suitable inscriptions are placed throughout the cemetery. The funeral of your relative was conducted with full military honors in the Chapel of the station. A Chaplain of the same religious faith conducted the service. At the grave a Firing Squad rendered a Salute to the Dead and a Bugler sounded taps.

There can be no more suitable resting place for a man who served his country than in the company of those Comrades with whom he spent an important period of his life serving his country, and in a plot which will be maintained perpetually by the Government.

This information will convey to you the appropriateness of burial of an Ex-Soldier, Sailor or Marine in the Government cemetery and will in some measure help comfort you in your loss.

Carl A. Neves, M.D.
Manager

Sisters Hospital in Hot Springs where Sverre got his first job in the U.S.

ENDING UP IN MINNEAPOLIS

I did not have any reason to stay in Hot Springs, South Dakota, after my father died, so I began to make plans to go back to Norway. I quit my job and left on a bus to Minneapolis, Minnesota. I got a room to rent and was looking for work. I paid $10 to get a job. The job was to put large barrels onto a truck. I could not do that heavy work and walked off the job and lost my $10.

A few days later I saw a sign—Bus Boy Wanted. I was thinking it had something to do with a bus. I applied for the job and got it. But the job had nothing to do with a bus. The job was to take clean dishes into the dining room and bring dirty ones out to the dishwasher.

Sverre in his suit after coming to Minneapolis, Minnesota.

I found out there was a place where I could learn English. I went there and took evening classes. There I met many Norwegians who were doing the same thing. I was learning English fast now, and changed my mind about going back to Norway.

I rented a different room from a really nice Swedish lady. The bathroom was in the hall and everyone on the floor used it.

At the restaurant where I worked, the day cook needed someone to help him during the noon hours so he asked me to help him. I said, "Yes, but I'm not sure how much help I can be." He said, "I will teach you and the boss said it was fine with him."

So at noon I started cooking for about one and a half hours every day. I was learning the menu and doing okay. Sometime later the night cook quit so I asked for the job. I told the boss I needed someone to help me over supper hour and I could finish the rest. They closed at 2 a.m. Well, it went fine and I was now the night cook. After a while, they hired a new night cook. I was now working mostly in the day time and was preparing most of the food they used each day. I did most of the ordering for the food they needed. Things went very well for a long time.

All dressed up and taking a leisurely walk in downtown Minneapolis.

THE LETTER FROM MY NEIGHBOR AND FRIEND

One day I got home from work and I got a letter saying that my neighbor and friend had selected me to join the United States Army. I did not understand all that so I took it to my boss at work and she laughed. She said I had been drafted into the U.S. Army. I had about a week to get ready and put everything I owned into a suitcase. My boss said I could store it at the restaurant where I had worked.

I left for Kansas City, Kansas, for basic training. This was December 10 in 1950. The Korean War had just started, so the U.S. Army needed more troops. Well, I got my training there and then I was sent to Seattle, Washington, to board a troop transport ship headed to Japan, and from there to Korea.

JAPAN

JAPAN'S NATIONAL ANTHEM

JAPANESE

君が代は
千代に八千代に
さざれ（細）石の
いわお（巌）となりて
こけ（苔）の生すまで
Kimigayo wa
Chiyo ni yachiyo ni
Sazare-ishi no
Iwao to narite
Koke no musu made

ENGLISH

May your reign
Continue for a thousand, eight thousand generations,
Until the pebbles
Grow into boulders
Lush with moss

Japan Flag.

Waiting for orders after our arrival in Japan.

COOKING ON THE BOAT

When we left Seattle, Washington on the way to Japan, they kept calling my name over the loud speaker. I was to report to the kitchen to cook. I was too seasick to cook, so I thought to myself, "They cannot find me here, since there are over 2,500 soldiers on the ship in uniform and we all kind of look alike."

But after two days they said they would put me in jail if I did not show up.

So I decided it was time to show up.

I went to the kitchen.

They said, "You are going to fry fish."

They gave me two grills to fry on, three feet by two feet and that really kept me busy. After the fish were done cooking, I had to put them in containers to keep them warm. I did this for about two to three hours. Then I had to go to the food line and help serve the soldiers. The smell of the food made me kind of sick and also the movement of the ship didn't help. Then we had to get ready for the next meal.

I also had the privilege to go into the supply room where I could get oranges and apples to take with me back to my bed. I cooked for about three to four days, then someone else was called up to cook. I was getting lots of experience cooking for many people at the same time, and that came in handy later in my cooking experiences.

I would give some of my apples and oranges to some of the soldiers who were really seasick. They could not stand regular food. I was seasick myself, so I knew how they felt.

I made many friends but after we left the ship, I never saw them again. But maybe some of them remember the part-time cook on the troop transport ship in 1951.

THE FIRST WEEK IN JAPAN

We landed in Japan, near Tokyo, where we got to sleep in regular barracks. In those days we all smoked. I did, too. They were having problems with fires. Soldiers would fall asleep in their beds with a cigarette burning, so by every bunk bed they had an empty coffee can with water in it, so it would be easy for the soldiers to put out their cigarettes. They had two guards (fire guards they were called) walking around to make sure nobody had fallen asleep with a cigarette in their hand.

We were called out two times a day to listen to hear what company we were being assigned to. We were all going to Korea, but with different companies.

My name was called out to cook in the big kitchen at the camp. They fed soldiers there all day long, from 6 a.m. to 8 p.m. This was the biggest kitchen I had ever seen. My job was to stir the soup. I had to walk up a ladder where there was a platform around the soup pan. The soup pan was almost 12 feet high and 5 feet wide, all the way from the floor up to the platform where I was standing. It was vegetable soup. I had a big wooden stirring spoon. This was a hard job.

They fed 5,000 soldiers each day. How many cooks they had, I don't know, but it was a lot. This was one of the biggest kitchens in the Army. The food was pretty good. I did this for two days, then my name was called out to be sent to Korea.

KOREA

KOREAN

Donghae mulgwa Baekdusani mareugo daltorok
Haneunimi bouhasa urinara manse

Refrain

Mugunghwa samcheolli hwaryeo gangsan
Daehan saram daehaneuro giri bojeonhase
Namsan wie jeo sonamu cheolgabeul dureun deut
Baram seori bulbyeonhameun uri gisangilse

Refrain

Gaeul haneul gonghwalhande nopgo gureum eopsi
Balgeun dareun uri gaseum ilpyeondansimilse

Refrain

I gisanggwa i mameuro chungseongeul dahayeo
Goerouna jeulgeouna nara saranghase

ENGLISH

Until that day when Mt. Baekdu is worn away and the East Sea's waters
run dry,
God protect and preserve our country!

Refrain

Hibiscus and three thousand ri full of splendid mountains and rivers;
Koreans, to the Korean way, stay always true!
As the pine atop Namsan Peak stands firm, unchanged through wind
and frost,
as if wrapped in armour, so shall our resilient spirit.

Refrain

The Autumn skies are void and vast, high and cloudless;
the bright moon is like our heart, undivided and true.

Refrain

With this spirit and this mind, let us give all loyalty,
in suffering or in joy, to the country's love.

South Korea Flag.

KOREA

This land of deep valleys and high mountains is bordered by China to the North and Japan across the Korean Strait and the Sea of Japan to the East. Korea was for many years ruled by the Chinese or the Japanese invaders.

After the defeat of Japan at the end of World War II (1939–45), Korea was left with no government of its own. The Soviet Union agreed to help the Koreans who lived north of the 38th parallel, a line that divides North Korea and South Korea. The United States agreed to help South Korea. At that time the United States and the Soviet Union were Allies.

On June 25, 1950, North Korea crossed its 38th Parallel border into South Korea (The Republic of Korea) with Russian supplied arms, tanks and air support. President Truman committed U.S. troops to South Korea on June 30, 1950. General Douglas MacArthur was put in command of the U.N. troops on July 7, 1950.

It was a bloody war and over 53,000 soldiers, including 8,000 Americans are listed as MIA and are assumed killed by the North Koreans. Over 33,000 U.S. soldiers lost their lives in the Korean War.

A ceasefire for the Korean War was signed by General Clark on July 27, 1953.

THE NEVER-ENDING FIGHT FOR FREEDOM

I spent about a year in a combat zone during the Korean War. These are some of the things that happened to me during the Korean War. These are true stories.

Sometimes I would tell a story to people and they would say to me you should write them down and that is what I have been trying to do. Norwegian was my first language. I do not write English very well, so my daughter, Rose Marie, has been helping in correcting my spelling. She also is a writer and has written some books.

As a soldier, it can be very hard to be away from civilization for such a long time. You get homesick sometimes and wish the war was over but that is only wishful thinking. You are there to do a job and you do the best you can under the circumstances. We all know we are fighting for freedom.

I lived under the Nazi German Occupation in Norway for five years so I know what it is like to not be free. You have to stand up and fight for freedom. It is not easy sometimes. I do believe the U.S. has done a lot for people all over the world to be free and I was proud to be in the U.S. Army fighting for freedom.

I believe having a strong army and a good government is the key to freedom and also helps smaller nations to keep their freedom.

*Sverre Waagen in his
U.S. Army uniform.*

USS Lenawee *(APA-195) transport ship taking soldiers to Korea.*

LANDING IN KOREA

We left the camp in Japan and were on our way to Korea. We boarded an old train with no windows because they were all missing. We went through Hiroshima, the city that was bombed with the atomic bomb. It had nothing left, only black soot everywhere. I was glad when we finally made it through the city.

It was 1p.m. when the train stopped and we were going to get something to eat. They opened the door and gave us each two cans—one with cold beans and one with hard bread. This is what they call sea rations. We were hungry so we ate it. I had a tough time getting it down. We were on the train another four hours. Then we had to board a troop transport ship. There were about 2500 soldiers on the ship. We slept twenty-four in each section. It was very compact. There were 6 feet high bunks on the boat sides and the same on the front end with four sections for a total of 24. You had to sleep with your M1 rifle and your steel helmet. We were now sailing away from Japan across the Yellow Sea to Korea. It took about a week.

We stopped out some distance from the Korean shore. They had some kind of fish net ladder but really heavy that they put over the side of the ship. We had to climb down this with our M1 rifle, steel helmet and ammunition belt. It was very daring. There were high seas, the ship was moving and very scary. Many of the soldiers were crying. They were scared to death. At the end of the shipside was the PT boat. We stepped into the PT boat, the sides were very high and we could not see over them. We were landing right below Seoul. The North Koreans had pushed the Americans all the way South to the sea so they had to leave by ship.

Our job was to cut the North Koreans off right below Seoul. The PT boat opened outwards in the front and we got ashore easy enough. The

Marines had landed there before us. So we had to clean up any resistance that was left. Some of the Army companies went south. The ones I was with went north toward the 38th parallel.

That night we slept in Seoul's biggest schoolhouse. All we got to eat was sea rations. The beds we slept in were bunk beds, two high and made of wood. One board was two inches thick; the next was half inch with no mattress. It was much better to sleep on the ground.

The next day we were on our way North. The North Koreans were on the run. The weather was cold and raining. We finally stopped. I was assigned to a soldier who was there already and had a foxhole. The artillery company was right behind us. They were firing constantly. We had a tent over the foxhole. Every time they fired the top of the tent swayed back and forth. It was like sleeping in a mud hole. The dirt kept falling into the fox hole.

WE FELT SORRY FOR THE CHILDREN

During my first guard duty in Korea, we had moved north from Seoul for about two days. We stopped to get some food. The Officers told us not to give any of our food to the civilians. At first we did not know what they were talking about.

We got our food and started to eat standing up. But all of a sudden there were women who had ten to fifteen children with them, ages from 2 to 8 years old. The women would stand back but the children would come forward with old cans and beg for food. It really hit you what kind of life these children had, it spoiled your appetite and you could not eat. So you gave some of the food to them. They smiled and thanked you.

Well, this is what happened to the people when their country was at war. We felt sorry for them, but there was nothing we could do for them.

We were soldiers and our job was to fight the enemy. And we hoped we would win so things would get better. This is the way we looked at South Korea now, hoping we could stop the war. We, the soldiers, would be a big part of ending the fighting.

We were to stay there over night. There was a big tent set up that had hay on the ground and we were supposed to sleep in it. The tent was full of soldiers. I went in there and went to sleep. Most of us were asleep the minute we laid down. We were all tired.

We got very thirsty, but we had our water canteens with us so it was okay. Our throats got very sore from the dust when we were on the move like this, so nobody talked. We all just kept to ourselves. And we did not know any of the other soldiers, since the next day we most likely would be fighting alongside different soldiers. We would most likely be sent to different companies and have different duties.

GUARD DUTY IN ENEMY TERRITORY

It was already dark out—about 12 midnight—when I was woke up and told to stand guard. It was a circle 50 yards from the tent. I got my ammunition belt, my steel helmet, hooked my bayonet on and grabbed my M1 rifle. I had to walk about 50 yards back and forth, and it was very dark.

There were lots of bushes nearby and in the dark it seemed like they were moving. I was very scared, but I kept my cool. I had not had guard duty in enemy territory before. I had my rifle in firing position and my finger on the trigger at all times. This duty was very scary especially for my first time guard duty in enemy territory. I made it through the night. Then, I had to get the next soldier to stand guard. I had pulled my two hour guard duty and it sure was different then the guard duty we practiced at training camp.

The next morning we went North again toward the 38th parallel. It was very dry and the dust was bad. We were all as dirty as we could be from the dust. There were not any roads, just trails. There were lots of trees and bushes on the mountain sides.

Suddenly, we were hit by some small arms fire. We fired back, but if we hit anything, we did not know because we did not stop to check it out. But they did not fire at us anymore and they did not hit any of us either. We kept moving, we were going for the 38th parallel.

A few peaceful minutes before the next attack.

Always watching for enemy attacks.

COOKING FOR THE OFFICERS

I was sent to the HG & HG (Headquarters & Headquarters) Company as a cook. The head cook took one look at me and said, "I do not like you. I am going to get rid of you as soon as I can. You will be at the front line in no time." In about five days I was sent to cook for the officers and anyone he sent there only lasted about a week and then was sent to the front line. Of course, I did not know that, but I found that out later.

Well, I now had to feed about forty officers and the Colonel. I did my best and for some reason they liked the way I did things. The war went on and I was still feeding the Officers. It was kind of nerve wracking to be around all the Officers all the time, but I got used to it.

The old cook, who sent me to cook for the Officers, was finally sent back to Japan and he never came back. I guess he was kind of crazy. He had been in combat too long, but he did not get his wish. I was still cooking for the officers. Well, that is what sometimes happens when you are in combat too long.

LETTERS FROM HOME

We had mail calls off and on. Most of the letters I got were from Alice Haase. She was my girlfriend when I left the States. She would write often and tell me what she did every day. It was nice to hear from her and what was going on back home. It took my mind off the war, and it would keep me thinking I might make it home again, someday. I would get some letters from my relatives and friends in Norway, too.

From the letters I got, I knew they all were keeping track of the Korean War. They all were wishing the war would be over soon and that I would be getting home soon. When I got letters from home, it always helped me to go on.

Many soldiers did not get any letters and they felt bad, so many times we would let them read some of our letters. This would make them cheer up and we would talk. The younger they were the harder it was for them.

It was a little easier for me because I had left Norway when I was 19 years old. I came to the U. S. and could not speak the language so I had been through tough times before. But what I was going through now was a lot worse. To be under artillery fire all the time was very nerve wracking. You did not know if you were going to get hit or not. You were not safe anywhere.

It reminded me of being in Norway during the 2nd World War. Mainly, the times we went to Ålesund to shop and there was an air raid so we had to go to the air raid shelter or bomb shelter. It usually lasted about one hour. You could hear the explosions but you did not know how close they were. The only difference then was you could hear the sirens stop which meant it was over, for that time anyway.

The difference here was there were no sirens going off telling you it was over for now. In Korea, you did not know how long it would last.

Sometimes it went on for days. Some soldiers went crazy from being on the front lines and had be sent to the hospital in Japan for treatment.

No matter how many friends you made in the Army, letters from home were always welcome. One time I got a letter from Gimitro's Ham and Eggs, where I used to work. They all had wrote a little note and this really made me feel good. So for people who know someone serving in the Army, far away from home, sending a letter really makes their day.

Alice Haase, Sverre's girlfriend (and future wife)
back in Minneapolis, Minnesota.

THE RAINY SEASON

The First Calvary Division had been on the front line for quite some time. We were pulling back for some rest, about four to five miles back away from the artillery range. One day, we could not get all the stuff from the Officer's tent on the truck, so I was supposed to stay back to watch the stuff until they came back with the truck. But, they did not come back with the truck that night so I went to spend the night in my fox hole.

The next morning I woke up and I walked to the front line. I came across the telephone man. He asked, "What are you doing on the front line?" He recognized me from the kitchen. I did not know this was the front line. He said, "They were attacked last night and had to pull back about two miles." I had slept through it all, that was how tired soldiers got some times. He called my unit and they sent a truck over right away. I made it back there and started my regular duties.

In Korea, they have what is called, the rainy season. That night we camped in a hillside. I dug my fox hole and got to sleep about midnight. When I woke up about 3 a.m., my foxhole was full of water and only my head was above the water. It was raining very hard. I had to use my steel helmet to scoop the water out. Everything I had was wet. I had some problems with my M1 rifle because it was wet, so I took it all apart and dried it out because that was one thing you definitely had to have in working condition.

The following day, we moved back about a half mile from the front line, but we always remained in range of the artillery fire. We were there for a week and it rained every day.

One of Sverre's bunkers in Korea.

Bunker and foxhole buddies—Sverre and Scott in Korea.

MY BIRTHDAY—NOVEMBER 9, 1951

When we were pushing north towards the 38th parallel, the weather was fair but cold. We had to cook in the army truck when it was moving. There was no road, it was like a trail they were following and it was not easy to cook, but any food was better than eating sea rations.

Today it was wieners. We stopped for a while when we were about one mile from the 38th parallel and set up camp, so the soldiers could eat. I was in charge of the Officer's tent.

We dug our fox holes by the time it was very dark. It was very quiet, but about midnight all Hell broke loose. The North Koreans had surprised us with artillery fire. We scattered everywhere. I ended up between a little hill and a tree. I laid there all night while artillery shells landed all around us. There was no place to go and it was too dark to go anyplace anyway. I prayed all night. When it got light out, I had to go to the Officer's tent and make them breakfast. I cooked for about 40 Officers. I made it there and got food ready, but only 20 showed up. The rest were killed. An artillery shell had hit a large tent where the officers were gathered. That night we lost at least half of our company.

The place where I was laying earlier that night, between the little hill and tree, no longer had a hill. It was flattened to the ground and pieces of artillery shells were everywhere, but I had not been hit.

The reason I remember this night so well, is it was my birthday, November 9, in 1951.

KOREAN WAR 1951—THANKSGIVING DAY

We had moved forward over hilly territories all day. It was snowing and raining on that particular day and I was in charge of the truck containing everything from the Officer's tent. We finally stopped and I got an order to set up the Officer's tent. It was cold and wet, and it was tough walking in half snow and half dirt. We got the tent set up but it was not easy to do in this kind of weather, and this was a large tent.

Then the Colonel said we had to move it and what the Colonel says, you have to do. He said we were in the enemy's line of fire.

We moved the tent over about 200 yards. When we got it all up again, the Colonel said we had to move it again. This would be the third time to put up the tent. We did move it and put it up again for the third time.

We now had to start to cook the turkeys. We had a kerosene stove to use, but had 25 turkeys, so we had to start two days ahead of time to get it done. We worked day and night because we had to cook the other meals for the men, too, and then go back to the turkeys again. We had 250 soldiers plus 40 Officers to feed. That was lots of hungry men to feed. The army goes all the way out for the Thanksgiving and Christmas meals. Other times the food could be pretty lousy.

We did not get much sleep during this time. We also had to dig our fox holes in the rain and snow. It is hard to sleep in a fox hole when you are cold and wet.

Artillery fire was coming at us all the time, but they landed about 150 yards short of us. But you never know when they will come closer.

The Thanksgiving dinner went well. The artillery shells never reached us. On that Thursday, the Lord let us eat in peace. But I will never forget that day as long as I live.

THE DAY I GOT SICK

I got sick. It was too hot. I had a high fever and felt really sick, so they said I had to go to the Field Hospital. So a jeep truck came to pick me up. In the back it had two beds on each side of the truck, but they were all full and one soldier was lying on the floor so they threw me on the floor beside him. The floor was metal, so it was hard. There were no pillows or blankets. They never said we were going to a Field Hospital about four hours away. There was no road, it was only a trail over very hilly territory. This was in July and the temperature was in the nineties. It was a very rough trip, my knee and back were very sore from lying on the hard floor of the truck. I said to myself, "This is a torture trip, I wish I was back in my fox hole."

Well, after a long four hour drive we finally got there. It was a large army tent. I walked to the tent and they said to just lay down on one of the army cots. A doctor came to check me out. He said, "You have Malaria." He gave me some pills and said, "Go to sleep."

There was no fan and it was very hot. But I finally got to sleep. I woke up about five o'clock and I was so thirsty. There was one soldier that was in charge of the tent. I asked him for some water. He said, "There is a bucket of water at the other end of the tent outside. Go and get it."

I was too dizzy to stand up and walk, so I crawled all the way over there. It was a garbage can with water in it, and there was a dipper inside to use to get water out of it to drink. The water was very warm. But it was water. I drank some and crawled back to my bed.

The doctor came in the morning and gave me some more pills. My breakfast was a can of sea ration. Well, I was there for four to five more days and then the doctor said I could go back to my Army unit. I was glad I could leave that hospital. I got a ride with some army trucks back to my Army unit. I was told you could get Malaria from a mosquito bite. I did recover pretty good from the Malaria. But my back and knee were sore from the truck ride for a long time.

No matter how sick I got I did not want to go back to that hospital. But this was in a war zone so things were not very good. I do not think I will ever forget that ride to the hospital.

A SCARY EVENING

It had been great for about two days, but the soldiers were all on the edge and restless. We were camped out on a hill. We had crates of ammunition boxes that were empty, so they had set them up in the hillside trying to make it look like an outside movie theater. We were going to see a movie. They were trying to make us relax. It was a very nice day in July, the temperature was in the 90's. We had to wait until it got dark which was about nine o'clock at night. The movie was very interesting and we were all wrapped up in the movie. I cannot remember what it was all about though. But, I do remember it was interesting.

We all had our M1 rifles with us and ammunition belts on. The guards also had at least six grenades with them. They had them on all the time. Since I was a cook, I did not have to carry them all the time.

In about the middle of the movie, there was an explosion. Then at least seven or eight more. The movie went off and we scattered all over. We all were thinking it was enemy fire. It was dark and we did not know what was going on. I finally ended up in my fox hole. Everybody ended up in their positions. But there were no more explosions.

The ones that were wounded got bandaged up and they were okay. I was sitting next to the ones that got wounded. But I did not get hurt. We all wondered what had happened.

Well, this is what happened. The soldier next to me had taken his grenade belt off and laid it by his feet. During the movie he somehow had kicked the safety pin out of the grenade and the grenade went off. I guess the empty ammunition boxes took the hit and we were saved.

This was the first time and the last time I went to any movie they set up. I liked movies but this was too dangerous. But good luck was with us this time.

Hanging out with my buddies and our guns outside our tents.

Checking out the communication tent.

ROUNDING UP THE CIVILIANS

There were many civilians who were scattered around in the hillsides. They did not have any place to go and they were hungry and dirty. We rounded them up in one place where we had the army trucks parked.

We sprayed them down with some kind of chemicals because they had many different kinds of bugs on their bodies. We could not have them bring the bugs to the camp where they were going. We tried to keep things there as clean as possible. At the camp, they would get a shower and different clothes. They also got food to eat.

Often, I would be sent down to the place where they first were gathered up. I had been there many times before. But this one day, I had just left to go back to camp and gotten about half a mile from there, when there was a big explosion. A land mine had exploded and many of the people were killed. I was just lucky that it did not happen the day I was working there.

There were lots of mines in that area. The soldiers, who were supposed to find the mines and get rid of them, had missed one.

I guess I was just lucky. Again.

Korean civilians.

THE BIG MEETING

They were very busy days during the war. We were constantly under artillery fire and often soldiers would get hit. Then they were sent back to a tent hospital about ten miles behind the lines. It was not much of a hospital, but that's all we had. At the hospital, they were given some pills and bandages. If they were still in bad shape, they were sent to Japan.

One day we received orders to get a bunker set up for a meeting. It was for the Generals along with some commanders from the United Nations. I remember there was a Greek General and an Italian General, about eight Generals all together. Most of them came by helicopter.

They needed extra guards for inside the bunker and to my surprise I was picked for that job. It was not a job you liked to do, because all the "Brass" made you nervous. But it was an order and you had to do it. For a job like that you had to stay at attention for two hours, but it was also an honor to be picked to do it. I was glad when it was over. The meeting went fine. I got to hear a lot of information about the war. But I could not repeat it to anyone.

ORDERED TO THE FRONT LINE

One day I was told to go to the front line. We had to pull back about a mile and we had lost quite a few soldiers. At the Headquarters we had been ordered to reinforce the front lines. The Lieutenant Colonel now was in charge of picking the men to go, he came and told me to get ready to go by 3 p.m. It was about 9 a.m. This was the kind of news you hated to get.

The Colonel was a nice man. He said to me, "You are doing such a good job feeding the Officers that I hate to let you go, but be ready to go at 3 p.m."

I cleaned my M1 rifle, filled my ammunition belt and got some grenades. I put my bayonet on the ammunition belt and I got my blanket ready. These were the only things you carried with you, when you were on the front line. I was ready to go. I had fed the Officers for the lunch meal and my job in the kitchen was over for now.

Many things went through my mind, when I was waiting for the Colonel to pick me up to go to the front line. What kind of battle was it going to be? Was it going to be hand to hand with fixed bayonet? Was this the end? It is funny how many things come to your mind in a situation like this.

The Colonel arrived at 2 p.m. and said, "You do not have to go. I got someone else to go in your place." I did know the soldier he had picked to go in my place.

He had brought me a 50 caliber machine gun and said, "Get this ready to operate and sandbag it in place, you are in charge of this." I had not fired a machine gun since I was back in basic training in Kansas.

"We are expecting a big battle tonight," the Colonel said. "We are very short of soldiers so we have to pull double duties. We are getting reinforcements but we do not know when they are coming. See you at breakfast."

Well, that night I got no sleep. But to our advantage the North Koreans did not manage to break through the lines. I served breakfast the next morning, but I was still in charge of the machine gun until the replacements arrived about a week later.

The soldier, who took my place on the front line, got shot up pretty bad and was sent back to Japan for hospital treatment. I heard he was doing okay.

I managed to make it through that week. Luckily, we held our position and the North Koreans had to retreat.

FEEDING THE SOLDIERS AT THE FRONT LINE

It was the cook's job to feed the soldiers in emergency situations. It had been a very tough time in the war. The men on the front line had been pinned down for days, and they were desperate for food. We at the Headquarters had been ordered to cook food and go up to the front lines to feed them. So we did. We cooked the food and brought it to the men. We put the cooked food in military containers to keep it warm.

We came to the front lines in four trucks under heavy artillery fire from the North. We put the trucks about 50 yards apart and set the food under the trucks. The soldiers had to be ten yards apart and they stopped at each truck to get the food. I was under one of the trucks serving the food to the soldiers. It took about two hours to get this done.

The cooks from the Headquarters were lucky we did not get hit. The men from the front lines did not get hit either. Sometimes you can be lucky even when fighting in a war. It was a tough time for all of us, but we were U.S. soldiers and when we had a job to do, we did it. It didn't matter what it was, it was just another day for a soldier at war.

TAKING A PRISONER

On the day I took a prisoner, one of the guards woke me at 4 a.m. just as they did every morning. That was one of the jobs they had to do. It was a beautiful morning, not too hot yet. I went to the kitchen and started the coffee cooking. That was usually the first thing I got ready. There was always someone asking for coffee, especially the guards who were trying to stay alert.

I was usually the first one to get to the kitchen tent. The other cooks came later about 4:30 a.m. We had to carry our M1 rifles on us at all times, even when cooking. It was a nuisance and it got in the way while I was cooking. It weighed 9 ½ pounds. But those were the orders.

I heard something outside of the tent, so I got my rifle ready and went outside to check it out. To my surprise, it was a North Korean soldier, fully armed. I took a step back. I did not know how many more were there. I did not see anymore.

I had my rifle pointed right at him and ordered him to drop his rifle and put his hands up. This was serious business, if he did not, I would have to fire my rifle. I did not know for sure if there were more North Koreans hiding out nearby the tent. To my surprise, he dropped his rifle and put his hands up. Just as I had ordered. I looked around but did not see or hear any other North Korean soldiers.

Now what was I to do? I had a prisoner, and I had to cook breakfast for the soldiers. I hollered as loud as I could, "Guard!!" I did this a few times. Then one of the guards came and I handed over the prisoner to him. I was relieved because now I could go back to cook breakfast for the soldiers.

As I was preparing breakfast, I heard more noise outside the tent. I thought to myself, "Was it more North Koreans?" But when I looked out I saw many of the Officers and the Colonel. They were questioning the prisoner and I heard they got lots of good information from the prisoner to help us with the war. I do not know how the North Korean soldier had managed to get in the middle of our camp and what he was up to. But maybe I saved many lives by unarming him and taking him prisoner.

I felt proud that I had gotten the upper hand on the situation and most of all had done my job as a U.S. Army soldier. I went back to work and tried to forget the whole thing. I was the only cook I know of who had taken a prisoner.

BACK TO JAPAN

Occupation soldier in Japan during the winter.

Barracks in Japan.

THE EARTHQUAKE IN JAPAN

Sometimes while in Sappora, Japan where we were occupation soldiers, we could get a pass to stay in a hotel overnight, just to get away from the military for a day or so. I decided to do that. The hotels were really cheap in those days, but the hotels did not have beds, they only had mattresses on the floor. To go to the bathroom you had to go out in the hall and everyone used the same one. There was no stool only a hole in the floor and you had to squat down and do what you had to do.

I had about two beers downstairs in the bar before I went to bed.

I was tired and went to sleep about 3 p.m. My mattress moved from one wall to the other and the building was shaking. I woke up in a hurry and wondered did I have too many beers or what? I looked out the window and there was a stone chimney moving back and forth. I had to hold on to the window, I was so unsteady on my feet. I wondered if that chimney was going to fall down and come through the window.

All kinds of things kept going through my mind. I was sure someone had spiked my beer or how else could I get that drunk from only two beers. Well I made it back to my mattress, laid down and did fall back asleep.

I woke up in the morning and got ready to go back to camp. I looked out the window and saw the chimney was still standing but thought it really was some kind of beer they had here in Japan. The next time I will have only one. I had to be back to camp by noon and take over my cooking shift, after all I was the Head Cook.

Well, I got back to camp okay, got my cooking uniform on and went to the kitchen to take over my shift as it started at noon. All my cooks were there.

They asked, "Where were you last night when the earthquake hit?"

"I was in town at the hotel. So that was what it was," I answered.

Then I told them what happened to me. "The mattress went back and forth from one wall to the next and I could not stand up. I thought I had too much to drink or someone had spiked my beer. But now I know this was not the case at all."

They were all laughing at me and asked, "Haven't you ever been in an earthquake before?"

I said, "No, this is my first time."

Some of those soldiers were from California and there they have earthquakes often. Japan has earthquakes often, too. When I was there we had three earthquakes, but this was the first one for me.

Occupation soldier in Japan (left).

Cook duty in Japan.

BACK IN THE UNITED STATES

GETTING BACK TO MINNEAPOLIS IN 1952

When I got back to Minneapolis in 1952, I was at the bus station downtown and I did not know where I was going to stay. I did not have any relatives there. My sister, Gerd, had moved to Seattle when I was in Korea. She was the only relative I had in this country, so I would have to get a hotel room.

I tried to make a phone call to get a hotel room but my nickel kept coming back from the pay phone. I tried many times but the nickel just kept coming back. I could not figure out why the phone would not work!

An older lady, who had been watching me, came up to me and said, "You have to put a dime in, the rate has gone up while you were gone." She could see by my uniform that I had been overseas serving in the war.

I said, "Thanks very much. I did not know."

"That is understandable," she said and left.

I put a dime in and the phone worked now, thanks to the lady.

I got a hotel room and went to bed right away. I had traveled a long time and was very tired.

The next morning I got up and went to 9th and Hennepin to Gmitro's Ham and Eggs. That is the place I used to work before I was drafted into the Army. The food was very good. No more sea rations for me. I did not see anybody I knew. It was all different waitresses and cooks. I had been gone a long time.

The weather was nice, so I walked around town for a while. I was still in the Army, I was just on leave. In a week or so, I had to report to the Army camp in Wisconsin to an engineering company. After that I would be discharged in about 30 days.

I went to see my old land lady and she was happy to see me. She

SURVIVING NORWAY'S NAZI OCCUPATION AND THE KOREAN WAR

was Swedish and a very nice lady. "Do you have any rooms for rent?" I asked.

"When do you need it?" she asked.

"In about 30 days," I said.

"You can have your old room back. It will be vacant then," she said.

"That sounds really good," I said.

"You just come and see me when you get discharged," she said.

"Good bye," I said and left. How lucky could I be?

COULD HAVE BEEN KILLED IN WISCONSIN

When I got back from Korea and Japan, I was sent over to report to a Wisconsin Army camp to join an engineering company. We had to build bridges over a river. I had never done this before and it was quite an experience. This was an exercise to pretend like we were in combat. We could build a bridge in about two hours.

Then we had to act like we had to attack the enemy. This was the exercise. Only they were firing live ammunition over our heads. So we had to crawl on our stomachs so we did not get hit. Well, I was one of the front soldiers. But the artillery was too close. They were learning, too!

Since I was the front man and had been in combat before, I knew this was not right. I signaled for the soldiers not to go forward and by that stopped the whole exercise.

I was later told I did the right thing. How many lives I saved, I don't know. I just knew since I had been in real combat for a long time, I was not going to be killed in a U. S. Army exercise in Wisconsin.

You hear lots of times about U. S. Army exercises that go wrong and soldiers get killed by accident. I felt proud of myself for having the guts to stop the exercise. I felt I was a good U.S. Army soldier. I did what was right for everyone there that day.

WAR HUMOR

THE BATTLE OF PORK CHOP HILL

We were dogged in on top of Pork Chop Hill. It was a muggy day. I heard a noise. I got out of my foxhole. I saw them coming up the hill. I hooked my bayonet to the front of my rifle. I knew it was going to be hand to hand battle. I used the butt of my rifle to swing to the left and then to the right. I looked around and the other soldiers had gone down the hill. I realized I was up there all by myself. I fought that much harder, this was life or death. And I tell you up to this day I have never killed so many mosquitos at one time.

OLE AND THE MN NATIONAL GUARD

Ole . . . A born salesman.

Ole, the smoothest-talking Norskie in the Minnesota National Guard, got called up to active duty. Ole's first assignment was in a military induction center.

Because he was a good talker, they assigned him the duty of advising new recruits about government benefits, especially the GI Life Insurance, to which they were entitled.

The officer in charge soon noticed that Ole was getting a 99% sign-up rate for the more expensive supplemental form of GI Insurance. This was remarkable, because it cost these low-income recruits $30 per month for the higher coverage compared to what the government was already providing at no charge.

The officer decided he'd sit in the back of the room at the next briefing and observe Ole's sales pitch.

Ole stood up before the latest group of inductees and said, "If you haf da normal GI Insurans an' yoo go to Afghanistan an' get yourself killed, da governmen' pays yer beneficiary $20,000. If yoo take out da supplemental insurans, vich cost you only t'irty dollars a mont, den da governmen' got ta pay yer beneficiary $200,000!"

"Now," Ole concluded, "Vich bunch you tink dey gonna send ta Afghanistan first?"

WAR MEMORIBILIA

U.S. Army First Cavalry Division Emblem.

6·25전쟁 50주년
THE 50th ANNIVERSARY OF THE KOREAN WAR

A letter of gratitude received from the Republic of Korea on the 50th Anniversary of the Korean War (in both English and Korean).

June 25, 2000

Dear Veteran

On the occasion of the 50th anniversary of the outbreak of the Korean War, I would like to offer you my deepest gratitude for your noble contribution to the efforts to safeguard the Republic of Korea and uphold liberal democracy around the world. At the same time, I remember with endless respect and affection those who sacrificed their lives for that cause.

We Koreans hold dear in our hearts the conviction, courage and spirit of sacrifice shown to us by such selfless friends as you, who enabled us to remain a free democratic nation.

The ideals of democracy, for which you were willing to sacrifice your all 50 years ago, have become universal values in this new century and millennium.

Half a century after the Korean War, we honor you and reaffirm our friendship, which helped to forge the blood alliance between our two countries. And we resolve once again to work with all friendly nations for the good of humankind and peace in the world.

I thank you once again for your noble sacrifice, and pray for your health and happiness.

Sincerely yours,

signed
Kim Dae-jung
President of the Republic of Korea

감사 서한
Letter of Appreciation

대 한 민 국
THE REPUBLIC OF KOREA

존경하는 참전용사 귀하

　6·25전쟁이 발발한지 반세기를 맞아 세계의 자유 민주주의와 대한민국을 수호하는데 기여한 귀하에게 진심으로 감사드립니다. 아울러 고귀한 생명을 바치신 영령앞에 무한한 경의와 추모의 뜻을 표합니다.

　대한민국이 오늘날의 자유 민주주의 국가를 유지할 수 있도록 귀하께서 보여주셨던 불굴의 신념과 진정한 용기, 그리고 거룩한 희생정신을 우리는 가슴속 깊이 간직하고 있습니다.

　특히 귀하께서 50년전에 몸으로 실천했던 자유민주주의 이념은 이제 새로운 세기, 새 천년을 맞아 세계 인류의 보편적 가치가 되었습니다.

　이에 6·25전쟁 50주년을 맞이하여 귀하의 명예를 드높임과 동시에 과거 혈맹으로 맺어졌던 귀하와의 우의를 재다짐하고자 합니다. 아울러 인류의 발전과 평화를 위해 세계 우방들과 함께 노력해 나갈 것입니다.

　다시 한번 귀하의 숭고한 헌신에 깊이 감사드리며 행운과 건승을 기원합니다.

　감사합니다.

2000년 6월 25일

대 한 민 국 대 통 령　　김 대 중

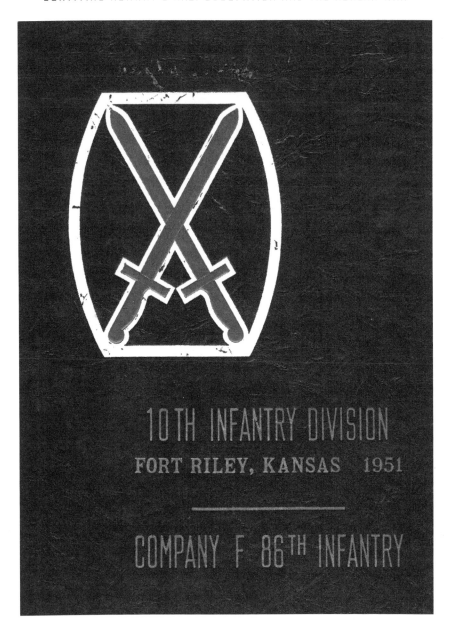

Private
RAY V. VIKLUND
Pleasant Grove, Utah

Private
LLOYD J. VOTRUBA
Hemingford, Nebr.

Private
JASON K. WAAGE
Groton, S. Dak.

FOURTH PLATOON

Private
SVERRE WAAGEN
Minneapolis, Minn.

Private
DALLAS D. WAGNER
Culbertson, Nebr.

Private
RUSSELL F. WALTER
Klamath Falls, Oreg.

53

Fort Riley 1951 yearbook.
(Sverre Waagen bottom left corner.)

After Duty Hours

Clean up duty. (Sverre Waagen top picture, lower right.)

CHAIN OF COMMAND

Commander-in-Chief
President Harry S. Truman

Secretary of Defense
General George C. Marshall

Secretary of the Army
Frank Pace, Jr.

Secretary of the Air Force
Thomas Finletter

Secretary of the Navy
Francis P. Matthews

Chairman, Joint Chiefs of Staff
General Omar N. Bradley

Army Chief of Staff
General J. Lawton Collins

Air Force Chief of Staff
General Hoyt S. Vandenberg

Navy Chief of Staff
Admiral Forest P. Sherman

Commanding General, Fifth Army
Lt. Gen. Stephen J. Chamberlain

Commanding General, Fort Riley
Maj. Gen. Lester J. Whitlock

Commanding General, 10th Infantry Division
Brig. Gen. James E. Moore

Assistant Division Commander
Brig. Gen. Marcus B. Bell

Chief of Staff, 10th Infantry Division
Col. T. W. Parker

68

U.S. Military Chain of Command 1951.

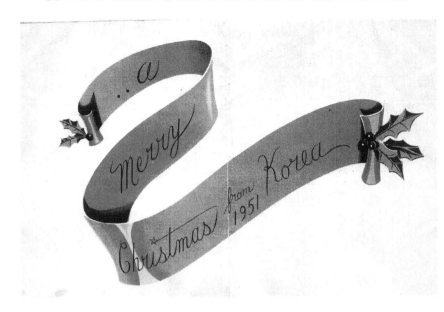

Sverre Waagen's 1951 Christmas card sent to his mother in Norway.

Sverre Waagen

was born in 1927 in Gursken, Norway, to parents Gyda and Gabriel Waagen. His father came over to America in 1911 and became a U.S. citizen by serving in the U.S. Army in WWI. Sverre came to America in 1947 as a U.S. citizen after Norway's Nazi Occupation and WWII ended. He then was drafted into the U.S. Army and spent approximately a year in Korea as a soldier in the First Cavalry Division of the U.S. Army along with several more months in Japan as a U.S. Army Occupation soldier.

The U.S. Army trained him to be a cook and he was a restaurant owner for many years. He can still be found cooking new recipes today, such as Lutefisk Hotdish. He is proud to be a life member of the American Legion.

Sverre has traveled back to his home in Norway many times throughout the years. Norway and his heritage have remained a large part of his life. He has been a member of the Sons of Norway for many years and the Norwegian Glee Club for over fifty years.

After returning from the Korean War, he married Alice Haase in 1953 and they raised six children. He and his bride of sixty-one years currently reside in Clearlake, Minnesota, surrounded by woods.